FROM THE HEART
TO MY
Friend

TO: Mary

FROM: Diane 12/25/07

forever and ever

FROM THE HEART
TO MY

Friend

VICKY HOWARD

Andrews McMeel
Publishing

Kansas City

ISBN: 0-7407-4185-3

Library of Congress Control Number: 2003112410

04 05 06 07 08 WKT 10 9 8 7 6 5 4 3 2 1

Page design by Rex Howard
Type design by Desiree Mueller

Preface

Nellie Howard was an artist and a teacher in Kansas in the early 1900s. She was also my husband's beloved grandmother. As a teacher, she collected volumes of Victorian postcards from her students. And Nellie treasured a very special collection of cards given to her by her friends. She lovingly preserved them in an antique jewelry box that is now a family heirloom. As an artist, I greatly admire the talented illustrators whose work adorns these beautiful postcards. Many of the friendship cards are decorated with floral motifs that conveyed special meanings of their own. To the Victorians, pansies represented kind thoughts and remembrances. Roses were symbolic of love, joy, and grace. Violets expressed faithfulness. Blue periwinkles portrayed new friendship, and lily of the valley signified a return to happiness and serenity. Richly colored and incredibly detailed, the cards are masterpieces of the "Golden Age of Postcards," the period from 1898 to 1918. These rare images, many over one hundred years old, celebrate friendship and are to be cherished—just as we cherish our friends.

*A friend is a rare
book, of which one
copy is made.*

—*From Friend to Friend,* 1913

ow wonderful friendship is! It is hard to imagine life without it,

and our desire for it is universal. Even so, friendship is a word that is

difficult to define because it means so many different things to each

of us. And each friendship is as unique as the personalities involved.

Our friends are the foundation of our lives, remaining steadfast as

life continually changes around us. Friends console us and cheer us.

Heartfelt talks with friends can diminish any problem we might have, bringing us laughter when we need it most. And in joyous times, happiness is magnified when it is shared with friends. As has often been said, friendship doubles its joys and divides its sorrows.

In this book I share Nellie's friendship postcards as well as favorite images from my own collection. Many of the poems were selected from antique books on friendship that were first printed in the early 1900s. The wisdom and emotion conveyed by the heartwarming verses ring true today, as friendship is a steady glow that never fades with the years. It is my hope that the reflections on friendship in this book will be a celebration of the true treasures of life—friends.

What Is Friendship?

Friendship is the essence and the aroma of life, distilled from human hearts that find in each other the understanding of the other's needs. It is this understanding that opens wide the doors of friendship and lets the heart pass through.

—Edwin Osgood Grover

Illustration by
Frances Brundage, 1908

One of the most wonderful qualities of true friendship is to understand and be understood.

—*From Me to You*, 1913

A friend is someone who reaches for your hand but touches your heart.

—Kathleen Grove

Frances Brundage

A friendly word, a friendly glance,

A friendly deed, a friendly gift—

And even the saddest heart will dance

And the weariest eyes uplift.

—John Jarvis Holden

Printed in
Germany, 1912

A GOOD DEED
IS NEVER LOST.
HE WHO SOWS
COURTESY, REAPS
FRIENDSHIP
AND PLANTS
KINDNESS,
GATHERS
LOVE.

—Richard Brooks, *I Have Called You Friends*, 1913

Printed in
Germany, 1912

All these are elements of happiness—love of nature, acquaintance with the wide earth, and abiding friendships.

—Charles W. Eliot

Printed in
Germany, 1910

Nothing is more common than the name of friend, nothing more rare than true friendship.

—From Friend to Friend, 1913

Who knows the joys of friendship?

The trust, security, and mutual tenderness,

The double joys where each is glad for both?

Friendship, our only wealth,

Our last retreat and strength,

Secure against ill fortune and the world.

—Nicholas Rowe

from friends gather half their joys.

—Young

The desire for friendship is strong in every human heart. We crave the companionship of those who can understand. We long for the presence of one who sympathizes with our aspirations, comprehends our hopes, and is able to partake of our joys.

—Elbert Hubbard

Printed in Germany
by John Winsch, 1911

Printed in Germany

Of all the best things
upon earth,
I hold that a faithful
friend is the best.

—Meredith

The glory of friendship is not
the outstretched hand, nor the kindly
smile, nor the joy of companionship;
it is the spiritual inspiration that
comes to one when he discovers
that someone else believes in him
and is willing to trust him
with his friendship.

—From Friend to Friend, 1913

OUR FRIENDS SEE THE BEST IN US, AND BY THAT VERY FACT CALL FORTH THE BEST FROM US.

—Black

Printed in
Germany, 1908

Printed in Saxony
by Raphael Tuck
& Sons, 1908

A true friend is an inspiration as well as a comfort, not so much by what he does for us as by what he incites us to do and be, because of his example, his deeds and his ideals. What others see in us to admire or be grateful for is a result of what our friends are and of what our friends have induced us to strive to become.

—*I Have Called You Friends,* 1913

Where true love bestows its sweetness,
Where true friendship lays its hand,
Dwells all greatness, all completeness,
All the wealth of every land.

—Josiah Gilbert Holland

Coffee trade card by
W. F. McLaughlin & Co.,
Chicago, 1896

A Loving Thought

Love is the sacred
link which binds
Hearts joined by
friendship firmer still;
Who once has felt it,
in it finds
Joys which his soul
with pleasure fill.

—*The Book of Friendship Verse*, 1924

The greatest
healing therapy
is
friendship
and love.

—Hubert Humphrey

$\mathcal{L}$ove—a deep interest in another being—what a charm there is in it, inexpressible, indefinable. It is the light of Life.

—William Ellery Channing

A friend is dearer
than the light of heaven;
for it would be better
for us that the sun
were extinguished,
than that we should
be without friends.

—Saint John Chrysostom

Printed in Germany
by Raphael Tuck & Sons, 1908

*Friendship is precious,
not only in the shade, but in the
sunshine of life; and thanks to a
benevolent arrangement in things,
the greater part of life
is sunshine.*

—Thomas Jefferson

Printed in
Germany

The friendly raindrops
   lend their aid
      To every blade of grass;

The flowers in all the fields
   are swayed
      Where friendly breezes pass.

The brook that slides
   along the glade
      Sings many a friendly air;

'Tis endless friendship
   that has made
      The splendid world so fair.

—S. E. Kiser

FOR OLD TIMES SAKE

Many kinds of fruit grow upon the Tree of Life, but none so sweet as friendship.

—Larcom

WISHING YOU HAPPINESS

The better part
of one's life consists
of his friendships.

—Abraham Lincoln

Series printed in Germany, 1912

Sweet flower—
that speaks of friendship true
Will bring my special wish to you:
May health and happiness be near
To bless each day throughout the year.

—Nineteenth-century postcard

MANY HAPPY RETURNS

Illustration by Frances Brundage, 1908

Instead of a gem, or even
a flower, cast the gift
of a lovely thought into
the heart of a friend.

—G. Macdonald, *Forget Me Nots
for Kind Thoughts*, 1911

Printed in Germany, 1908

We were meant to radiate the perfume of good cheer and happiness as much as a rose was made to radiate its sweetness to every passerby.

—Unknown

Illustration by C. Klein;
printed in Germany, 1910

HAPPINESS
IS A PERFUME
YOU CANNOT POUR
ON OTHERS
WITHOUT
GETTING A
FEW DROPS
ON YOURSELF.

—*Just Being Happy*, 1913

Illustration by C. Klein;
printed in Germany, 1909

*More hearts
than we dream of
enjoy our happiness
and share
our sorrow.*

—George William Curtis

Illustration by
Frances Brundage, 1910

Beautiful friendship, by sun and wind; durable from the daily dust of life.

—Phillips, *From Friend to Friend*, 1913

Life is short, and

we never have too much

time for gladdening the

hearts of those who are

traveling the journey

with us.

—Amiel, *Just Being Happy*, 1913

The hill is long and rugged,

But just around the bend

Might be a sunlit meadow

Or the handclasp of a friend.

—*Benedict's Scrapbook*

*O*ur friends are among the choicest possessions life has bestowed upon us, and we should use the greatest possible care in preserving them. It is our duty to exert every effort to retain old friends and to make new ones. Someone has truly said that great is the fellowship along that highway of life known as friendship's road.

—Unknown

Woolson Spice trade card, 1893

COPYRIGHTED 1892 BY THE KNAPP CO. N.Y.

You call me friend ...
But do you realize
How much the name implies ...
It means that down the years,
Through sunshine
*   and through tears,*
There's always someone
*   standing by your heart.*

—Hilda Butler Farr

Printed in Germany by
Raphael Tuck & Sons

American Girl illustration by
Pearle Fidler LeMunyon; printed in the USA, 1920;
courtesy of Rose Mary Green

The happiest moments of my life have been in the flow of affection among friends.

—Thomas Jefferson

Friendship is the golden thread that ties the hearts of all the world.

—Evelyn, *From Friend to Friend*, 1913

Printed in Germany

Too my Valentine.

The world is wide and the world is grand,

And there's little or nothing new,

But its sweetest thing is the grip of the hand

Of a friend that's tried and true.

—Unknown

Illustration by
Ellen H. Clapsaddle, 1914

Trade card, Home Insurance Co. of New York, 1896

$\mathcal{G}$ive me a friend,

and my youth may depart

$\mathcal{B}$ut still I'll be young

in the house of my heart,

$\mathcal{Y}$es, I'll go laughing

right on to the end,

$\mathcal{W}$hatever the years,

if you give me a friend.

—Unknown

BE HAPPY; LET WHO WILL BE SAD,
THERE ARE SO MANY PLEASANT THINGS,
SO MANY THINGS TO MAKE US GLAD,
THE FLOWER THAT BUDS, THE BIRD THAT SINGS;
AND SWEETER STILL THAN ALL OF THESE
ARE FRIENDSHIP AND OLD MEMORIES.

—M. C. D., *Just Being Happy*, 1913

Printed in Germany, 1911

*L*ife is made sweet because of the
friends we have made,
And the things which in common we share.
We want to live on, not because of ourselves,
But because of the people who care.
It's in giving and doing for somebody else
On that all life's splendor depends;
And the joys of this life, when you've
summed it all up,
Are found in the making of friends.

—Edgar A. Guest

Be assured, dear friend,
Memory will never forget
The hours I have
spent with you.

—Unknown

Trade card, John Church Co., Cincinnati, Ohio, 1893

There is no friend like the old friend
who has shared our morning days,
No greeting like his welcome,
no homage like his praise;
Fame is the scentless sunflower,
with gaudy crown of gold;
But friendship is the breathing rose,
with sweets in every fold.

—Oliver Wendell Holmes

The only rose without thorns is friendship.

—Madeleine de Scudéry

Count your garden by the flowers,
Never by the leaves that fall;
Count your days by golden hours,
Don't remember clouds at all;
Count your night by stars, not shadows,
Count your life by smiles, not tears;
And with joy through all your lifetime,
Count your age by friends, not years!

—Unknown

Trade card, Lion Coffee, 1894

It's great to have a friend like you

as I journey through this life;

I thank you now for all you do

to banish doubt and strife.

—Unknown

Printed in Germany, 1910

I'd like to be the sort of friend
that you have been to me;
I'd like to be the help that you've
been always glad to be;
I'd like to mean as much to you
each minute of the day
As you have meant, dear friend
of mine, to me along the way.

—Edgar A. Guest, *A Heap O'Livin'*, 1916

*What a thing friendship is—
world without end!*

—Robert Browning, *Poems of Home Life*, 1876

Printed in Germany, 1913